STYLE & SUBSTANCE

HOW TO CREATE A COMPELLING BRAND

A Guide for Women Who Want to Build
Their Confidence, Their Brands and Their Bank Accounts

LIZ DENNERY SANDERS

STYLE & SUBSTANCE

Cover and interior design by Michelle Sanchez
BareMade Studio

ISBN-13: 978-0-692-99181-7

For more information, please visit www.shebrand.com
Or email hello@shebrand.com

DEDICATION

Behind every successful woman is a wolf pack of female friends cheering her on, saying, "OMG, you're a star," and "girl, you can do this," even when she felt like, perhaps, she could not.

To Susan Hyatt, Rachel Rodgers and Tara Martin, thank you for your endless love and support and for always being at the ready to travel the world and drink champagne with me. You are diamonds in a world filled with cubic zirconias.

And to Alexandra Franzen, your love and encouragement knows no bounds. Thank you for believing in me and my mission and helping me use my voice like no other. You are my unicorn.

TABLE OF CONTENTS

"

Find out *who you are* and do it on purpose.

DOLLY PARTON

INTRODUCTION

I have been working with brands for more than half my life. What began as a few internships at advertising agencies and public relations firms during my college years, and a stint as a publicity coordinator for Warner Bros. Pictures, eventually turned into working on advertising and marketing campaigns for powerhouse fashion brands like Ralph Lauren, Oscar de la Renta, Prada, Versace, and more at Harper's Bazaar during my time in New York City.

Every campaign felt like a puzzle to be solved—a puzzle filled with questions like, "What does this company stand for?" "What's the central promise they want to make to their consumers?" "Is it the promise of adventure, luxury, serenity, peace of mind, excitement, or innovation, or maybe it's something else?" "Is that promise being expressed clearly and consistently?" "Do consumers see it, feel it, and believe "it"? "If not, how could we make this happen?" I loved seeing how the right language, photography, graphics and so many other elements could come together to make a company's promise—its brand—shine through.

In 2000 I started my own consultancy, which evolved into a full-fledged agency by the time I moved to Los Angeles in 2002. Over a 10-year period, we worked with large, multi-million dollar brands, like Escada, Dior, Hale Bob, Anastasia Beverly Hills, Storksak, Paulina Maternity, Cedars-Sinai Medical Center and Elyse Walker, as well as high profile individuals like Serena Williams, Kelly Rutherford and Tiger Woods. We dressed everyone from Heidi Klum, Angelina Jolie, Sharon Stone, and Cindy Crawford, to Taylor Swift, Jessica Alba, Halle Berry, Penelope Cruz, Salma Hayek and Kendall Jenner in our clients' clothing and accessories.

After 25+ years of this work, here's what I've found: There are two things that the most successful brands have in common. First, they are very clear about who they are, what they stand for and who their dream client is—and they do a damn good job of communicating this to their audience over and over again. And second, they understand that the relationship—and connection—they build with their target audience and continue to maintain over time is the key to their success. These brands are clear, consistent and engaging, and they continuously deliver on their promise to their consumer.

I founded my second company - SheBrand - in 2009, because I felt that a lot of brands were doing a poor job of communicating with and marketing to women. I also wanted to help women entrepreneurs to build their confidence, their brands and their bank accounts. When women thrive, our society thrives and everyone wins.

As I started to work more closely with my female clients, I discovered that many of them had something in common: They felt completely overwhelmed when it came to building their brands.

Many of these women were swayed by bright, shiny marketing objects, and felt they needed to be everywhere and do everything in order to be successful. They'd spread themselves too thin and wind up feeling frustrated and exhausted. And with no more dollars in the bank.

Often, they would throw up a website, get on every single social media channel, sign up for dozens of networking events, order hundreds of business cards, and then dump all of those cards into the recycling bin two weeks later because the wording just didn't feel right. (A continual "Who am I?!" identity crisis.)

Many times, they'd spend hours fixating on microscopic stylistic details—like the exact shade of teal for a logo—while ignoring much more crucial action steps.

They'd purchase online classes and watch webinars that told them they needed to do more, more, more, and then wonder why they felt so overwhelmed and scattered. Or the reverse: they would be so paralyzed by all of the options available to them that they would freeze and do nothing.

Neither scenario is a good recipe for creating a strong brand—or a profitable business.

During meetings with these overwhelmed clients, I often found myself saying, "Let's get back to basics. Forget about your logo, your website or which color your next Facebook ad ought to be. Forget all of that for a moment. Let's start by laying a solid foundation for your brand. Let's figure out who you are, what you stand for, what you offer (and to whom), why you do what you do—and most importantly, the promise you're making to your consumer."

Once these foundational pieces have been sorted out, it becomes much easier to make business decisions—from the typeface for your logo, to the way you craft your weekly newsletter, to the content you share on your blog, to the way you dress for a speaking engagement, and all the other Brand Touchpoints that your consumer experiences.

But first—and I can't emphasize this enough—you need to begin with a solid brand foundation.

Many entrepreneurs don't know how to put this foundation into place, and can't necessarily hire a brand consultant to help them figure it out.

That's why I wrote this book.

My intention is to give you $10,000 worth of branding knowledge—and all of the questions and exercises I've used with my clients—in one simple workbook that you can work through on your own.

I created this book because I want you to succeed—madly. Like, over-the-top, insane, rock star success.

I want you to create your own raving fans.

I want you to get more of everything you want—more clients, more money, more opportunities, and the chance to help more people.

And whether you run a relationship counseling practice in West Hollywood or a dance studio in the West Indies, and whether you sell hand-knitted socks, face cream, essential oils or vitamin supplements, financial services, photography services or personal training sessions, or tickets to workshops and retreats that you host, the principles in this book apply to you.

With this book, you have everything you need to build your brand foundation—as long as you do the work. So take my hand, and let's get started.

I'll leave you with an interesting fact that's been backed up by research studies—most men overestimate their intelligence by about 10-20%. Meanwhile, most women underestimate their intelligence by about 10-20%.

Translation? You are more brilliant than you think. And the world needs what you have to offer.

You want a thriving business, fans who rave about you to their friends, and a distinctive brand that combines style and substance?

You can build all of that. You've got this.

With love + light,

Liz

PART ONE

SUBSTANCE

"

Overcome the notion
that you must be regular.
It robs you of the chance
to be *extraordinary.*

UTA HAGEN

WHAT IS A BRAND?

Pop quiz: what is a "brand," exactly?

Choose two of the following options:

  a. Your company logo

  b. The color palette on your website

  c. The way you dress and present yourself to the world

  d. The promise that you make to your target audience

  e. The way people perceive you, feel about you, and talk about you when you're not in the room

If you chose (d) and also (e), you're totally correct!

Visual components, such as your logo, website, business cards, Facebook page and the way you dress are all elements that contribute to the development of your brand in the mind of the consumer, but they are not in and of themselves, your brand.

A brand is a promise you make to your target audience, and ultimately, how your audience perceives you.

Red Bull promises energy.

Apple promises beautiful design.

Mercedes-Benz promises luxury and speed.

SoulCycle promises a sweaty, uplifting 45-minute workout.

Amazon promises ease, efficiency, and reliable two-day delivery.

Oprah promises growth, spirituality, and a pathway to your best life.

Michelle Obama promises style, composure and integrity with fierce support for women and girls.

Ellen DeGeneres promises lighthearted humor that's family-friendly.

It is what someone will get and/or how they will feel when they engage with you in some way—go to your website, read your blog, buy your products, hear you speak. In other words, a brand is the real estate you own in someone else's head—and you have to earn that real estate. Amazon business mogul, Jeff Bezos, once said, *"Your brand is what people say about you when you're not in the room."*

Imagine a group of women chatting about Beyoncé's latest album over brunch. What kinds of words would they use to describe Beyoncé? Probably words like *independent, talented, mother, businesswoman, activist, feminist, goddess.* That's our perception of Beyoncé, so that's her brand.

Now imagine a group of women chatting about Taylor Swift. What words would they use to describe Taylor? Most likely, words like *pop, fun, catchy, guilty pleasure, dancy-y, angsty, bold, feminist.* That's our perception of Taylor Swift. That's her brand.

The way people feel about you, perceive you, and talk about you when you're not in the room…that's your brand.

You might be thinking, *"Well, I really can't control what people think or how they feel about me or what they say about me, so….now what?"*

But actually, that's not true. You have a great deal of control over the way you're perceived. More than you might think.

If you want people to perceive you as *"bold, striking and surprising,"* you might choose to wear bold, bright colors instead of black, and you could surprise your clients with unexpected gifts in the mail. You could host a monthly salon dedicated to bold, striking ideas, create bold, colorful business cards and marketing materials and you could fill your office with strong, bold artwork, and so on.

This is how you affect the real estate with your name on it in the consumer's head.

Based on what you put forth into the world—your products and services, the language on your website, the way you speak and dress, the experiences you create for your audience, right down to the smallest details, like your Instagram posts and the fonts you choose—shapes people's perception of you.

Beyoncé does this masterfully. Do you think it's an "accident" that we perceive her as an independent, talented, feminist, and a living, breathing goddess businesswoman? It's no accident. Beyoncé is very strategic with everything she puts forth into the world, because she wants to build and sustain a very specific type of brand.

From the way she releases her music to the videos she makes to the clothes she wears and the images of she and her family she posts on social media—all are meant to create specific consumer perceptions. We perceive her a certain way, because she wants us to perceive her that way. She controls her brand—and you can do this, too.

The first step is getting clear about the promise you're making to your audience and how you want to be perceived. Start there, before you worry about your website or business cards.

A strong brand starts with a strong sense of who you are, what you stand for and what you most want to be known for. It's not about your logo; it's about your legacy.

Brand (n):

The promise you make to your target audience and the perception that is created in their minds through tangible and intangible touchpoints.

"

Be yourself.
Everyone else
is already taken.

OSCAR WILDE

WHY DO I NEED A BRAND?

In today's overcrowded and noisy marketplace filled with 24/7 newsfeeds, emails, messages and social channels, it takes a lot more than a pretty logo to stand out. Whether you're selling a product, service, workshop—or anything else for that matter—the best way to get your target audience's attention is to develop a relationship with them. And in order to establish a relationship, you first have to make a connection.

The best way to make an emotional connection with your target audience is to add value to their lives—consistently.

Brands that add value to their target audience through creative content, communication, experiences and overall generosity are positioning themselves for long-term success. Emotional branding is the connection people feel with brands that add value to their lives in some way.

There are many ways that brands connect powerfully with their consumers, but some of the most effective are to inspire, empower, entertain and educate. Every brand is different, but the most compelling brands usually incorporate one or more of these powerful actions into all of their Brand Touchpoints.

A great example of this is DryBar. They have exploded from one location to 82 locations in less than 10 years and have a raving fan base filled with loyal, repeat customers.

Aside from providing excellent service, they inspire, empower, entertain and educate their fans every single day. Their Instagram feed, for example, is filled with inspiring hairstyle and lifestyle ideas, empowering quotes, cute and entertaining photos (who doesn't love dogs wearing shower caps!), and more.

They state that they're "making the world a happier place, one blowout at a time" and their "happiness" mission is reflected in everything they do, from their sunny yellow color palette, to their product names, to their social media feed. They know exactly what type of emotion they want people to experience, and they're consistent in creating that emotion.

In other words, DryBar is doing an excellent job of weaving their main brand attribute and brand personality—"happy"—into all of their Brand Touchpoints.

If you want to stand out, attract your right clients, get your products and services out into the world in a powerful way, make an impactful difference or reach millions of people, then it's imperative that you create a strong connection with your audience.

With a compelling brand, consumers will flock to you, sing your praises to anyone who will listen and purchase your products and services.

WHAT IS A BRAND ATTRIBUTE?

A Brand Attribute is a word (usually an adjective) that best describes your brand.

What 3-4 words best describe your brand?

If you were the invisible woman at a cocktail party of friends, colleagues and people you don't know, and you overheard someone describing your brand to someone else, what are the three words you would most want them to use?

You selected these words for a reason. WHY are they important to you? WHY are they important to your target audience?

_____

_____

_____

_____

_____

_____

_____

Keep in mind, as you are building your brand, you will use your Brand Attributes as a filter. For example, if one of your attributes is "Inspiring," then you want to ask yourself, "How can I make my brand more inspiring?" In everything you do—from building your website to decorating your office, to developing your marketing materials and leading a workshop, you'll want to incorporate inspiration into everything you do.

Garcelle Beauvais
CLIENT SUCCESS STORY

When we began working with actress Garcelle Beauvais, she had a decent following on social media, including 100K fans on Facebook and close to 50K followers on both Instagram and Twitter. But she didn't own an online hub of her own and she wasn't yet clear on how to best communicate and control her brand. I've known Garcelle personally for years and she's always been a super dedicated mother, a great lover of fashion and a big supporter of women and empowerment. I told her that we needed to incorporate more of this—*more of her*—into everything she was doing.

We built a website that focused on her loves—family, fashion, supporting women and speaking her truth—and we started sharing more personal content on her social media platforms. In less than a year, Garcelle went from 100K fans on Facebook to well over a million, and more than 250K followers on Instagram. She started writing a "Mommy" blog for *People.com*, and was featured as one of the 50 Most Beautiful Women in the World by *People* in 2015. She is often featured on the pages of *USWeekly*, *InStyle*, *People* and countless other publications for her love of fashion.

Moral of the story: **when you get clear about who you are and what you bring to the table, and you share it with the world, the more your right audience is going to be drawn to you—and will engage with you.**

"

Life gives us choices…
you either grab on
with both hands
and just go for it,
or you sit on the sidelines.

CHRISTINE FEEHAN

DEEP DIVE QUESTIONS

Clarity is Queen when it comes to your brand. It allows you to communicate in a clear and easy manner, and ultimately will attract your right audience. Think of yourself as a lighthouse. The clearer you are about who you are, what you stand for, what you offer and who it benefits, the brighter your light at the top of the lighthouse will shine, and your ideal clients will be able to find you. The old saying, "A confused mind never buys," is true. If you are confused about your brand, your light will be dull and muddied, and you won't attract much of an audience.

So let's begin with an archaeological dig.

What are the three words that best describe your brand? Why did you choose these three?

_____

_____

_____

_____

_____

What do you currently like about your brand?

_____

_____

_____

_____

_____

What, if anything, would you like to change about your brand?

_____

_____

_____

_____

Who is your most ideal client?

_____

_____

_____

_____

_____

_____

_____

_____

_____

_____

_____

_____

What value do you provide to your clients/audience?

_____

_____

_____

_____

_____

_____

_____

HOW do you do it?

_____

_____

_____

_____

_____

_____

_____

_____

WHY do you do it?

_____

_____

_____

_____

_____

_____

_____

_____

What do you want your brand to be MOST known for?

_____

_____

_____

_____

_____

_____

_____

_____

What do you consider to be your Unique Message/Special Sauce/Genius?

What's your spirit animal—and WHY?

_____

_____

_____

_____

_____

_____

_____

_____

What's your personal theme song/anthem—and WHY?

_____

_____

_____

_____

_____

_____

_____

_____

What do others think of your company vs. what do you wish they thought?

In other words, how do others currently perceive you vs. how you want to be perceived.

_____

_____

_____

_____

_____

_____

_____

_____

What do people compliment you on most frequently?

_____

_____

_____

_____

_____

_____

_____

_____

_____

What do people come to you for when they need help? What do they thank you for most often?

_____

_____

_____

_____

_____

_____

_____

_____

What do you consider to be your three strongest characteristics? Why?

_____

_____

_____

_____

_____

_____

_____

_____

When someone at a party asks you what you do, what do you say?

How do you feel when you say it?

List three brands that inspire you *(at least one or more should be outside your industry)*

_____

_____

_____

_____

Of the three brands you listed in the last question, what are the main qualities/attributes that you admire most about each one? What are they doing RIGHT?

_____

_____

_____

_____

_____

_____

_____

_____

_____

_____

_____

_____

In your dream scenario, the *New York Times* (or *Wall Street Journal* or *Oprah Magazine*) writes a one paragraph blurb about your brand, what do they say?

"

As we work to create
light for others,
*we naturally light
our own way.*

MARY ANNE RADMACHER

PART ONE:SUBSTANCE

WHAT'S YOUR WHY?

What do you value most in life? Chances are, those in your target audience value some—or all—of the same things you do. If you can clearly define WHY you do what you do, and why it's important, you have a much better chance of building a clear, compelling brand and attracting a like-minded community of fans, followers and clients.

Simon Sinek, the author of the best-selling book, *Start with Why*, explains, "We're inspired by your dream, not your plan. The goal is to surround yourself with people who believe what you believe."

Starbucks CEO, Howard Schultz, once said, "If people believe they share values with a company, they will stay loyal to the brand."

It's important to define what you believe in and what you stand for, and make sure to promote those values in your brand.

People connect with passion, emotion, values and a great brand idea. How are you bringing your brand to life? How are you weaving your passion and excitement into everything you do?

Take some time to answer the questions on the following pages.

STYLE & SUBSTANCE | 39

WHY do you do what you do?

WHY should we care?

What do you want your brand to stand for?

How would you most like to help and inspire others?

If your clients were to describe your brand in just 2-3 sentences, what would they say about you?

_____

_____

_____

_____

_____

_____

_____

_____

_____

_____

_____

_____

_____

_____

_____

_____

_____

Seyie Design
CLIENT SUCCESS STORY

Seyie Putsure was already a successful interior designer when she approached me a few years ago. She was thriving, but she wanted to reach even more of her ideal clients. The interior design world is congested and highly competitive, and she wanted to stand out and differentiate herself from the rest of the crowd.

Before she entered the field of design, Seyie was an executive in NYC with luxury fashion houses Chanel and Dolce & Gabbana. She has a meticulous eye for art, style, architecture and fine craftsmanship, and brings this attention to detail into her design work. We defined her guiding principles, which are "luxury," "personalization" and "stylish function," and explored how these principles could be communicated throughout all of her Brand Touchpoints.

As we put together her Brand Handbook, we came up with a tagline of "where fashion meets function" for her design work, which epitomizes her special gift of combining these two distinct areas to create an extraordinary environment for her clients. For her corporate clients, we also created the phrase "interior branding" to express Seyie's ability to create a completely branded environment and ideal consumer experience for retail stores, spas, real estate developments, shopping malls and more.

Once Seyie was able to clearly communicate the ethos of her brand and what makes her style unique, she began to take on even more projects, from multi-million dollar homes just steps from the beach in Southern California, retail development projects in downtown Los Angeles, luxury retail boutiques and the backstage lounges for the 54th and 55th GRAMMY Awards.

Moral of the story: **Spend some time considering this question: "What makes my work different from my peers?" For example, Seyie isn't just an interior designer. She's a designer who used to work in the luxury fashion industry for iconic brands like Chanel. That's unique! What about you? What's the special twist (or perspective) that you bring into your work? Is there something you've done in the past (say, a previous profession, or a pivotal life experience) that gives your work a certain flavor today? Figure out what it is and express it, because this will help you to differentiate yourself from the rest of the pack.**

"

All you need is faith, trust, and a little bit of *pixie dust.*

30 WAYS I ADD VALUE

What is the value that your clients get from working with you? In other words, what are the benefits they receive and the results they achieve? List all things – big and small. Don't underestimate your value. It could be "I always make my clients laugh," or "I can find money in the tightest of budgets," to "my clients get clear about their goals in our first session together."

You get the idea. Now it's your turn.

1 _____

_____

2 _____

_____

3 _____

_____

4 _____

_____

5 _____

_____

6 _____

_____

7 _____

_____

8

9

10

11

12

13

14

15

16

17

18

19

20

21

22

23

24

25

26

27

28

29

30

"

We are each gifted
in a unique and
important way.
It is our privilege
and our adventure
to discover our own
special light.

EVELYN MARY DUNBAR

DISCOVER YOUR TRUE BENEFITS

When you speak to your clients' values—what they REALLY want out of life—and you give it to them, you'll be well on your way to building a compelling brand.

When you affirm their values and understand how they want to FEEL, you'll be able to speak with them about the things that they care about most.

There are two types of benefits—obvious benefits and TRUE benefits. When you uncover the TRUE benefits that clients get from working with you, you'll be able to connect with them at a much deeper level.

For example, if you are a Financial Advisor, some of the obvious benefits clients get from working with you might be:

- An understanding of certain financial products
- An organized spending plan/budget
- Learning how to budget and keep track of spending
- Clarity around their money and how they want to allocate it
- Sound investment advice

Some of the TRUE benefits might be:

- Peace of mind
- Financial independence/security
- Wealth/abundance
- Feeling smarter (when it comes to their money)

In other words, the TRUE benefits are how your client really wants to FEEL—it's the real thing(s) they value. It's your job to incorporate these TRUE benefits into your messaging and brand story. You can do this by describing your process (your WHAT and your HOW) and give examples of other clients (testimonials) who have achieved these results.

A few more examples of obvious vs. true benefits include:

Personal Trainer

Obvious Benefits:

Get fit

Gain muscle

Lose weight

More energy

True benefits:

Feel amazing in your skin/body

Feel more confident

Feel proud of yourself

Radiant health

Life Coach

Obvious Benefits:

Achieve specific goals like: "get a new job," "lose 10 pounds," "start dating again."

Have a cheerleader in your corner

Accountability

Improve your current circumstance

True benefits:

Feel happier and more satisfied

Feel empowered, like you're back in the driver's seat of your life

Feel optimistic about the future, knowing the best is yet to come

Create whatever it is you crave

Stylist

Obvious Benefits:

Clean out your closet

Get a new wardrobe

Feel better about your clothes

Get dressed more easily in the morning

True benefits:

Discover your own personal style

Feel truly confident in what you wear and how you look (more confidence all around!)

Look and feel your best and attract your ideal partner, job, opportunity etc.

Graphic Designer

Obvious Benefits:

Get a great logo

Get a beautiful website

Get professional-looking materials

True benefits:

Feel confident about spreading the word about your business and inviting people to check out what you do (no more "website shame!")

Feel excited to "put yourself out there" and share your information

Feel proud of the way your business looks and feels

Now it's your turn.

List five to ten of the obvious benefits of working with you:

List five to ten of the TRUE benefits of working with you (think values, feelings, experiences):

"

Nothing liberates our greatness like the desire to help, the *desire to serve*.

MARIANNE WILLIAMSON

WHO IS THE IDEAL AUDIENCE FOR YOUR BRAND?

To create a successful brand, you need to have clarity around your message and be able to communicate it to the right people. Your target audience includes your ideal clients and the people who influence them. Think about whom you would most like to work with and who would benefit most from what you have to offer. Also, who would be most attracted to your product or service?

Here's an exercise to get you started. This is a sampling of some of the demographics and psychographics you can collect on your target audience—feel free to add any additional information that's relevant for your brand:

Age

Gender

Career/Job Position/Title

Education

What do they do in their spare time?

Who do they hang out with and why?

What are their professional activities or organizations outside of work?

What social media platforms do they use—where do they hang out online?

What are their emotional fears, frustrations, disappointments?

What are their innermost hopes, dreams and desires?

Who are five people they admire most?

What do all of your ideal clients have in common?

What does your ideal client worry about? What keeps her up at night?

What would your client pay almost anything for? What does she value above all else?
(hint: this is usually a feeling or a particular state of mind)

Additional relevant information:

_____

_____

_____

_____

_____

_____

_____

_____

_____

_____

_____

_____

_____

_____

_____

_____

_____

_____

"

To be yourself in a world that is constantly trying to make you something else is the greatest *accomplishment.*

RALPH WALDO EMERSON

YOUR IDEAL CLIENT

Regardless of whether you are selling a product or service, you want to have a clear picture of your ideal consumer. And just as important as knowing who she is, is knowing who she is not.

Take a few minutes now to jot down the main characteristics of someone who is your ideal client, and then someone who is definitely NOT your ideal client, and would be a potentially bad fit for your product and/or service.

My ideal client IS:

_____

_____

_____

_____

_____

_____

_____

_____

_____

_____

My ideal client IS NOT:

_____

_____

_____

_____

_____

_____

_____

_____

_____

_____

_____

Rock Your Bliss
CLIENT SUCCESS STORY

When Mary Beth LaRue (a yoga instructor) and Jacki Carr (a goals coach) came to me, they had an interesting challenge…

They'd launched a business together called Rock Your Bliss, combining yoga and coaching to help people set intentions, shift into action, and achieve their goals. They'd built an enthusiastic fan base for their services, including the Rock Your Bliss online program and retreats.

The problem? They felt spread too thin and weren't sure where to focus their attention. Run more retreats? Do the same online program again? Or create a totally new service or class? They were working nonstop and yet the business wasn't as profitable as they knew it could be. They wanted to take it to the "next level," but the path forward didn't feel completely clear.

I encouraged them to bring things back to basics. We talked about what was most important to them, why they do what they do, who their ideal clients are, and the greater mission they have for the brand. I asked them, "What's the end-game for your clients?" In other words, after working with you, what's the result that you want your clients to get? Mary Beth and Jacki described the end-game as a feeling of bliss and excitement, which they summed up with this phrase: oh-my-god-i-love-my-life!

With that end-game in mind, we put together a Brand Handbook for the Rock Your Bliss movement. We looked at their digital platform and made sure their message matched their mission and that it was clear and consistent across all communication channels.

Once they got really clear on their values (community + authenticity + self-realization + play), and their end-game, they were able to weave these throughout all of their Brand Touchpoints and develop the types of offerings and content their community wanted most.

The response was spectacular. Since then, they have launched two successful online programs, five sold out retreats, dozens of speaking gigs, and most recently, the Rock Your Bliss podcast. Their brand is now more confident, compelling and "making shift happen" on the daily.

*Moral of the story: **Figure out your end-game. What's the destination you want your clients and/or customers to arrive at? This "destination" might be a dollar amount ("I earned an extra $10,000") or a feeling ("oh-my-god-i-love-my-life!") or a situation ("I've finally got my dream job!") or an achievement ("I ran my first 5K race!") or some other kind of destination.***

When people hire you, or purchase your programs and products, where are you taking them? Where does this journey begin—and where does this journey end? Figure out this end-game and communicate it clearly. This makes your brand so much stronger. It builds up your own confidence, too, because you know exactly what you're doing with your clients, and exactly how you're making their lives better.

"

We will be known
forever by the
tracks we leave.

BRAND TOUCHPOINTS

All of the tangible elements of a brand—logo, business card, website, marketing materials, products, etc.—work together to create the intangible: the perception that consumers have about your brand. All of your Brand Touchpoints give you the opportunity to consistently and effectively communicate your brand promise.

This is where you actually have quite a bit of control over how you are perceived—and it's also where you can incorporate more of your creativity, passion and values into your brand. Compelling Brand Touchpoints help your target audience engage with you in a way that's meaningful for them, too.

A great question to ask is, "how can I create a more sensory experience for my community?" In other words, what visual, verbal and olfactory experiences will help me better connect with fans, followers and clients.

Every Brand Touchpoint should reaffirm your brand promise and help to cement a consumer's perception of your brand. It also:

- opens the door to a conversation
- invites them in to participate
- adds value to their lives in some way
- inspires, empowers, educates or entertains in some way
- reminds people of who you are and what you stand for

Let's look back at the section in this workbook (page 25) where you wrote down your Brand Attributes. Re-write those top 3-5 words here:

As you read through the examples of Brand Touchpoints below, ask yourself, "how could I bring more of these Brand Attributes into everything I do?" In other words, if you wrote down "inspiring" as one of your attributes, continually ask yourself, "How can I be more inspiring in my blog posts, weekly newsletter, on my website, in my Instagram posts, in conversations with my clients, in the way that I dress, and all other touchpoints?"

Examples of Brand Touchpoints

Advertising campaigns	E-books	Personal wardrobe
Blog posts	Email communication	Press releases
Books	Event sponsorships	Public speaking
Brochures	Letterhead	Signage
Business cards	Logo	Social Media channels
Catalogs	Look books	Speeches & Interviews
Contests	Marketing materials	Text message campaigns
Color palette	Office environment/décor	Website
Coupons	Packaging	White Papers

When you create more frequency and interaction for your brand with ideal clients, you set the stage for an emotional connection. All of your Brand Touchpoints are the process of building a solid, likeable, compelling brand in the minds and hearts of your ideal clients.

Let's examine your current touchpoints and ways in which your customer interacts with you. Consider your list of 3-5 top Brand Attributes. For each touchpoint listed below, the question is…Are your attributes showing up clearly? If not, what could you tweak/change so that your attributes shine through?

Each touchpoint is an extension of you. For example, if you're a life coach, and one of your attributes is MOTIVATION, most likely, when people meet you, and spend time with you, they leave feeling motivated. So if you send out a postcard, if you send out a newsletter, if you send a gift to a client, if you lead a class or a webinar…all of those emails/gifts/experiences, etc. should remind people that your brand stands for MOTIVATION. The email/gift/experience should leave people feeling motivated, just like they feel when they're near you, even though you're not physically there. *Each touchpoint should make people feel the same way they feel when they're in your presence.*

The opposite scenario exists, too. Let's say you're a financial advisor, someone meets you and thinks you're so savvy, smart, informative and pulled together. But then, they go to your website, and it hasn't been updated since 2008. Links are broken, navigation is confusing, pages are disorganized and the only post on your blog says, "Hello world." From 2009. Now your potential client is thinking, "Hmmm, there's a disconnect here. Maybe this person isn't as savvy and put together as she seemed? Now there's mistrust and confusion. *And a confused mind never buys.*

Here is a list of some of the most common areas for Brand Touchpoints.

Under each one, list a few touchpoints you are currently using/engaged in—in other words, how are you currently using these in your business? How are you incorporating your Brand Attributes?

Logos/Design Elements/Colors

_____

_____

_____

_____

_____

Website(s)

_____

_____

_____

_____

_____

Physical Appearance/Personal Presentation

_____

_____

_____

_____

_____

Office Environment

_____

_____

_____

_____

_____

Email Communication

_____

_____

_____

_____

_____

Products & Services

_____

_____

_____

_____

_____

Customer Service

_____

_____

_____

_____

_____

Partnerships/Alliances/Sponsorships

_____

_____

_____

_____

_____

Now, from the previous list, or other areas that you have identified, choose three touchpoints you know you can create or improve upon to help your clients connect with you and more clearly understand what you do.

For example, you may decide to include two sentences about your brand values in your email signature or Facebook profile. Or you might choose to post a video on your website that explains why you do what you do, or perhaps hang a quote in your office that best represents your brand.

You get the idea. Now it's your turn—create three new, powerful touchpoints here:

Touchpoint #1:

Touchpoint #2:

_____

_____

_____

_____

_____

_____

_____

_____

_____

Touchpoint #3:

_____

_____

_____

_____

_____

_____

_____

_____

"

Your mission statement provides the why that *inspires* every how.

CHARLES GARFIELD

CRAFT YOUR MISSION STATEMENT

Oftentimes, we stay loyal to a brand because of their values. These values usually align with our own. And the companies (and individuals) who are the most successful over time are the ones who weave their values into all of their brand elements and create a strong emotional experience for their audience.

A mission statement declares your purpose, your big WHY—your raison d'etre. It clearly and concisely expresses who you are and your strongest intention for what you do. A vision statement, on the other hand, describes where you are going as a company. The two are often used together to describe a company's reason for existing and where they are heading into the future.

A few examples of company and individual mission statements:

Patagonia
Build the best product, cause no unnecessary harm, use business to inspire and implement solutions to the environmental crisis.

Harley Davidson
We fulfill dreams through the experience of motorcycling, by providing to motorcyclists and to the general public an expanding line of motorcycles and branded products and services in selected market segments.

Life is Good
To spread the power of optimism. Life is not perfect. Life is not easy. Life is good.

Facebook
To give people the power to share and make the world more open and connected.

Tesla
To accelerate the advent of sustainable transport by bringing compelling mass market electric cars to market as soon as possible.

Google

To organize the world's information and make it universally accessible and useful.

Whole Foods

Our deepest purpose as an organization is helping support the health, well-being, and healing of both people — customers, Team Members, and business organizations in general — and the planet.

MOMA

To collect, preserve, study, exhibit, and stimulate appreciation for and advance knowledge of works of art that collectively represent the broadest spectrum of human achievement at the highest level of quality, all in the service of the public and in accordance with the highest professional standards.

Oprah Winfrey

To be a teacher. And to be known for inspiring my students to be more than they thought they could be.

Richard Branson

To have fun in my journey through life and learn from my mistakes. In business, know how to be a good leader and always try to bring out the best in people.

Warby Parker

To offer designer eyewear at a revolutionary price, while leading the way for socially-conscious businesses.

Chanel

To be the ultimate House of Luxury, defining style and creating desire, now and forever.

L'oréal

Offering all women and men worldwide the best of cosmetics innovation in terms of quality, efficacy and safety.

KIVA

To connect people through lending to alleviate poverty.

Blue Apron
We make incredible home cooking accessible, for everyone.

Make-a-Wish
We grant the wishes of children with life-threatening medical conditions to enrich the human experience with hope, strength and joy.

Nike
Bring inspiration and innovation to every athlete in the world.*
*If you have a body, you are an athlete.

Whether you're writing a mission statement as a company as the brand—or as an individual as the brand—it's equally important to define who you are and what you stand for.

A few questions to get you started:

WHO are you?

WHAT do you do?

_____

_____

_____

_____

_____

_____

_____

_____

WHY do you do what you do?

_____

_____

_____

_____

_____

_____

_____

_____

_____

WHY is it important? (the work you are doing and/or the product(s) and services you are creating)

_____

_____

_____

_____

_____

_____

_____

_____

_____

_____

_____

_____

_____

A mission statement should be clear, concise and compelling—specifically directed at your target audience. But there are no rules. It can be one sentence, a few sentences or just two words, like AirBnB's mission, "Belong Anywhere," or TED's, "Spreading Ideas."

The important thing is that it is specific and shares your purpose and values.

Now it's your turn. Jot down a few words or sentences you might want to include in your mission statement.

You live your life on the cutting edge.
Let us get you there in style.

Elite Travel International
CLIENT SUCCESS STORY

A former luxury travel magazine editor and jet-setting journalist, Stacy Small founded Elite Travel International in 2005. Her goal? To reach a new generation of affluent travelers and provide them with incomparable, one-of-a-kind travel experiences.

When Stacy came to me, she wanted to revamp the Elite Travel International brand and create a new online platform that would disrupt the travel industry. She was unimpressed with the look of traditional travel advisor websites—most were stale and boring, and they all looked the same. She felt her current website was flat and uninteresting, too, and didn't represent her brand of luxury, style and meticulous attention to detail. She wanted her brand to evoke words like "originality," "sophistication," "elegance," and better represent her VIP clientele.

Pulling inspiration from the worlds of fashion, art, business and design, we created an elegant digital presence that looked nothing like the stodgy travel agency websites of the past. Because Stacy was willing to look outside her own industry for inspiration, we were able to create something completely unique, with a new spin and viewpoint.

Today, Stacy has established herself as the go-to luxury travel advisor for Silicon Valley executives, global entrepreneurs and the Hollywood elite. Instead of feeling the pinch of website shame—like she used to—now, she's confident sending clients and media to her online hub and feels that her brand is in complete alignment with her values and vision.

Moral of the story: **Look outside of your industry for inspiration. If you're a health coach, for example, don't study other health coaching websites and mimic them. Look elsewhere. Look at opera houses, iconic fashion labels, travel companies, and other businesses that aren't your direct competitors. That's where you'll find fresh ideas and concepts that nobody else in your industry is using.**

"

We're not meant
to fit in.
We're meant to
stand out.

SARAH BAN BREATHNACH

BRAND PERSONALITY

What are the feelings that you want your target audience to experience when they engage with your brand? What is the tone you want to set?

Your brand personality is your energy; it's your vibe. It's the feeling(s) your customers have when they engage with you and often continue to experience after they walk away.

It's also referred to as your brand tone or brand voice. Your voice is one of the keys to attracting your target audience and building a strong relationship with them.

While your brand personality can be conveyed in words, it's often the brands that express their voice through other means, such as images and experiences, that nail their personality.

For example, the women's clothing brand, Free People, shares beautiful images on their Instagram account (@freepeople) of women dressed in their clothing, traveling the world, hanging out near the beach and living a life of wanderlust and adventure. Their social media presence isn't just about the clothes they are selling, it's about the lifestyle that their client embodies.

You can bet that the women who follow Free People feel free, adventurous, feminine and bohemian whenever they engage with the brand—whether it's on their website, their Instagram feed or in one of their stores. That's the tone that the brand consistently uses for all of their touchpoints.

Your brand personality can be shared through your website copy, imagery, packaging, customer service, blog posts and everything you share on social media. Whenever possible, share your brand personality in all of your Brand Touchpoints.

Here are a few personality keywords to get you started. Which ones best describe your brand voice?

Accessible	Empowering	Humble	Serious
Altruistic	Encouraging	Imaginative	Sexy
Bold	Energetic	Inspirational	Silly
Calm	Entertaining	Intelligent	Smart
Caring	Feisty	Irreverent	Spiritual
Clever	Feminine	Luxurious	Sweet
Dependable	Friendly	Masculine	Warm
Edgy	Fun	Mysterious	Whimsical
Educational	Funny	Quirky	Witty
Elegant	Helpful	Rebellious	Zen

What are 3-5 words that best describe your brand personality? How do you want people to feel when they engage with you (or use your product or service)?

Brand Personality (n):
the way a brand speaks, behaves and engages. The energy of a brand and how the brand is experienced by its target audience.

PART TWO

STYLE

"

Fashions fade.
Style is eternal.

YVES SAINT LAURENT

WOMEN CONTAIN MULTITUDES

We're not just "one thing." We're many things.

A woman can be a devoted mother and a fierce businesswoman. A Harvard MBA graduate who obsesses over astrology and crystals (or the latest Tory Burch collection) in her spare time. A pop culture aficionado who also runs an award-winning architecture firm.

It irritates me when women get put into rigid boxes, when women are treated dismissively, and when our skills are underestimated (although never underestimate the power of being underestimated!)

All too often, in the media, women who unabashedly love fashion, beauty, makeup and other traditionally feminine pursuits are lambasted for being "shallow" or "air-headed." But this kind of snap judgement is tremendously short-sighted, and it isn't true.

Look at someone like Shakira, for example. She's done incredible philanthropic work, creating educational opportunities for children in her home nation of Columbia. She's a smart, generous philanthropist, a talented performer, and she loves wearing leather boots and midriff baring tops and Salsa dancing in her music videos. She's brilliant, kind, talented, an activist, an artist, energetic, fit, athletic and sensual. Shakira is a woman of style and substance. Not one or the other—both.

YOU are a woman of style and substance, too. And your brand, which is an extension of you, can comprise style and substance, beauty and intelligence, delight and depth. Both/and, not either/or.

The first half of this book was dedicated to substance—what you stand for, the value you offer, who you wish to serve, your mission statement, how you want to be perceived, how you want to improve your customers' lives and create positive change in the world.

The second half of this book is devoted to style—defining the exact look, colors, textures, and other aesthetic/visual qualities of your brand.

Style is more than just the clothes that you wear, of course—it's also the way you decorate your home and office, the photos you select for your Instagram feed, the way you interact with other people, every detail of your brand, down to the specific fonts you select for your logo and website.

By the end of this section, you'll have the information you need to put together a Brand Style Guide, which is a visual reference tool that will help you bring a consistent, recognizable style to everything you do. All the iconic brands that you love—Apple, Virgin Airlines, Chanel, Dior—they all develop "style guides" just like this, and now you can create a style guide of your very own.

"

Style is a simple *way of saying* complicated things.

JEAN COCTEAU

WHAT IS STYLE?

When we say, *"She's got such great style,"* what we really mean is:

"She's confident and comfortable in her own skin."
"She's not trying to copy anyone else."
"She's unapologetically herself, and expresses and adorns herself accordingly."

Style is not one-size-fits-all. It's different for every woman. Ultimately, style is knowing who you are—and expressing it with confidence.

Style is Grace Kelly's Hermès scarf tied around her head or her handbag, and the elegant, sophisticated way she carried herself into every room.

It's Anna Wintour's dark sunglasses and signature chin-length bob, conveying a "Let's get right down to business" boss-lady attitude.

It's Beyoncé's feminist lyrics and her stunning, semi-nude pregnancy photos, which defy the stereotypical notions of how a "good mother" should look and behave.

It's Diane Von Furstenberg's cool confidence, fierce support of women, and yes, her famous wrap dress—designed for women with places to be, and people to see, and who want to look chic and pulled-together in minutes.

It's Jennifer Lopez's midriff-baring tops, tropical, colorful prints and sky-high strappy stilettos—signifying that flirtation, boldness and sexuality do not have to expire after age 45.

Style is what we notice about someone and ultimately come to expect from them. It's an outward expression of who they are.

Style is self-knowledge and acceptance, and then knowing what to do with it. How you express yourself—from your personal and business interactions and how you treat others, to how you decorate your surroundings, and yes, how you dress—all contribute to your personal sense of style and how it is perceived.

So, who are you? What image do you want to project into the world? How do you want to be perceived by your clients, your customers, by strangers on the street? And if you don't have a well-defined personal style yet—how can you create one?

First, notice what captivates your attention. What lights you up inside? What piques your curiosity?

Life is filled with great style inspiration—art, books, design, food, travel, fashion—and gives you the opportunity to put your own personal twist on things. How you pull together your favorite elements, spin them together and make them your own defines your personal sense of style.

Ask yourself questions like:

What makes me feel confident when I put it on?

What feels inspiring and exciting?

What calls out to me in art, fashion, design, food, travel?

_____

_____

_____

_____

When it comes to my brand, what's the image that I want to project?

_____

_____

_____

_____

By answering these types of questions, you can begin to develop your personal sense of style—identifying your signature colors, textures, icons, shapes, silhouettes and other aesthetic elements.

Then comes the really fun part—infusing your style into everything you do, from the clothes you wear, to the décor in your home and office, to the images you select for your website, to the gifts you send to your clients (and the packaging, too), to your company logo, and every other place where people interact with you and your brand.

Diane Von Furstenberg once said that style is, "an effortless confidence in being yourself." I couldn't agree more.

Standing tall, using your voice, expressing yourself in everything you do (and wear), using your skills to create a positive impact in people's lives, and embracing what makes you different rather than simply following the crowd...that's true style.

When you've got that kind of confidence, it doesn't matter if you're wearing a $30 dress from a thrift store or a $4,000 couture gown—people will be drawn to you, inspired by you, and eager to engage with you.

When you take the time to cultivate great personal style and express it consistently, you won't get lost in the shuffle, you'll make a memorable and lasting impression.

HOW GREAT STYLE CUTS THROUGH THE CLUTTER

Your style is often what introduces you before you even open your mouth or walk into a room. The language of style is expressed through all of the senses and it is often how people get to know you—sometimes before they even meet you.

Great style is remembered and often copied.

Great style makes an imprint in someone's mind about you and makes it harder for them to forget you.

Memorable style creates memorable brands.

When it comes to a compelling brand, well-defined style is your calling card. It's what draws your "right" audience to you and let's them know that you are "kindred spirits."

Great style attracts your tribe and allows those not meant for you to fall by the wayside.

A compelling brand has compelling style. It's clear, well-defined and adheres wholeheartedly to its own distinctive approach.

"I have never known a really chic woman whose appearance was not, in large part, an outward reflection of her inner self."

– MAINBOCHER

"The only real elegance is in the mind; if you've got that, the rest really comes from it."

– DIANA VREELAND

"

What you wear is how you present yourself to the world, especially today, when human contacts are so quick. *Fashion is instant language.*

MIUCCIA PRADA

STYLE QUESTIONNAIRE

Start with what inspires you.

Lemon yellow?

The smell of freshly brewed coffee?

The lights of Paris?

Make a list here:

How would you describe your style?

_____

_____

_____

_____

_____

_____

_____

_____

_____

What are the three words that best describe your style?

_____

_____

_____

_____

_____

_____

_____

_____

_____

List 3-5 individuals whose style you admire and WHY?

Who is your style "spirit animal"? In other words, do you most admire Sienna Miller's style, perhaps with a dash of Kate Moss thrown in?

What would you like to change about your style—if anything?

What image would you like to project?

What do you want your style to say about who you are?

What are the first items you gravitate towards when shopping?

_____

_____

_____

_____

_____

_____

_____

_____

What are the most-worn items in your closet?

_____

_____

_____

_____

_____

_____

_____

_____

Favorite colors:

Favorite fabrics:

Favorite silhouettes:

Preferred fit (i.e. loose, body conforming, tailored etc.):

Please circle or highlight the colors/tones you wear most frequently:

Earth Tones	Bright + Bold
Neutrals	Pales + Pastels
Conservative + Monochromatic	Nontraditional + Daring
Jewel Tones	Contrasting Colors
Black is my favorite color	I can't get enough color

NOW, I recommend that you create a Pinterest board with images you find of your "style icons." You can make it a secret board if you choose. Select those pics you are most drawn to—many of them will be pictures of the people you mentioned above whose style you admire.

Once you've spent some time collecting photos, look through your inspiration board, notice the outfits, and pick a few words to describe the vibe of the looks. Are they mostly feminine and ladylike, or do they have a sporty or edgy look to them? This exercise will help you get a feel for the vibe you are most attracted to—and most likely want to convey.

"

Real style is never right or wrong. It's a matter of *being yourself* on purpose.

G. BRUCE BOYER

WHAT'S YOUR STYLE TYPE?

The most stylish women often choose a particular look and are consistent in how they dress. No matter what they choose to wear, they have found something they feel confident in and stick with it. That said, many women find themselves to be a combination of a couple of these "types," or, depending on their mood, a variation of one or the other. One style isn't better than the other—it really depends on your own personal taste and how you put your own stamp on it.

In the following pages are five of the most common style "types" and a few of the icons that best exemplify them.

CLASSIC

You will rely on chic, timeless pieces to get you through the most challenging of style conundrums. Instead of madly following every fashion trend, you prefer quality over quantity and effortlessness over fussiness. In your closet, we'll find simple staple pieces with an air of luxury, like a few crisp white shirts and silk blouses, a boyish blazer, a slim-cut trench coat and lots of navy, black and neutrals like sand, taupe and camel.

Your style sheroes are Audrey Hepburn, Jacqueline Kennedy Onassis, Carolina Herrera, Victoria Beckham, Jennifer Aniston and Gwyneth Paltrow.

Jennifer Aniston

Victoria Beckham

GLAMOROUS

You love sparkle, metallic, bold accessories and making a strong entrance. In your closet, we'll find gorgeous statement pieces like a faux fur leopard print coat, a slinky silk camisole dress, a slim fit tuxedo with satin lapels, a stack of cashmere sweaters and the perfect black leather jacket and leather jeans. You'll sip champagne any day of the week and your favorite thing to make for dinner is reservations.

Your style sheroes are Marilyn Monroe, Sophia Loren, Jennifer Lopez, Catherine Zeta-Jones, Halle Berry, Bianca Jagger and Iman.

Iman

Jennifer Lopez

LADYLIKE

Your polished style leans towards the classics, but you love the feminine flourish of a perfectly positioned scarf or bow and the understated ease of a ballet flat. In your closet, we'll find slim pencil skirts, silk blouses with feminine accents, floral dresses with a touch of lace, handbags with handles to wear over the elbow, and of course, the perfect Prada pump and Repetto ballet flat.

Your style sheroes include Grace Kelly, Kate Middleton, Diane Kruger, Olivia Palermo, Taylor Swift, Kiera Knightley, Reese Witherspoon and Kerry Washington

Kate Middleton

Diane Kruger

BOHEMIAN

You're a free spirit who loves color, sparkle, and light, diaphanous fabrics that move and flow freely. You don't like to be constrained by your clothes—no, you need comfort and movement for your own personal brand of self-expression. In your closet we'll find blue jeans, fringe, peasant blouses, romantic maxi-dresses, distressed leather, and probably beads and flowers, too.

Your style sheroes include Charlotte Rampling, Jane Birkin, Ali MacGraw, Diane Von Furstenberg, Kate Hudson and Sienna Miller.

Diane Von Furstenberg

Sienna Miller

EDGY

You're not afraid to experiment with avant-garde silhouettes and bold colors and you're always down for a tough look or an unexpected contrast. You prefer modern and sleek to feminine and frilly, but you have a way of mixing different styles to make them your own. In your closet we'll find studs, leather, spikey stilettos, lots of sharp edges and lots of black.

Your style heroes include Rihanna, Gwen Stefani, Madonna, Tilda Swinton, Chloe Sevigny and Katy Perry.

Gwen Stefani

Tilda Swinton

NOW IT'S YOUR TURN.

Most women don't have just one style type. We are often a blend of a couple of style types with a little bit of our own flair mixed in. That's what makes you interesting. You might be Classic and Ladylike with a heavy dose of Divine Feminine thrown in for good measure. Or perhaps you have an Edgy style with a splash of Punk Rocker Chic.

What are three or four words that best describe your personal style?
What's your very own style combo?

_____

_____

_____

_____

How would your best friend describe your personal style?

_____

_____

_____

_____

_____

_____

_____

"

Over the years
I have learned that
what is important in
a dress is the woman
who is *wearing* it.

YVES SAINT LAURENT

10 STYLE ESSENTIALS THAT EVERY WOMAN SHOULD OWN

Regardless of your own personal style, there are ten items that I believe every woman worth her fashion salt should own. They are the must-haves that will serve as the backbone of your wardrobe, and can easily be accessorized with items that suit your personal taste . Trends will come and go, but these are the items that will loyally serve you year after year.

1. LITTLE BLACK DRESS

This timeless piece can take you from the office to an evening on the town with the switch of a few well-chosen accessories. A simple, yet sophisticated black dress will serve as the perfect backdrop to a killer pair of colorful stilettos, a faux fur jacket or a statement piece of jewelry.

2. CLASSIC WHITE SHIRT

This perennial favorite will never go out of style. Paired with denim or a slim pencil skirt, the white button-down shirt exudes elegance. Just ask Carolina Herrera or Sharon Stone.

3. DENIM

There's a very good reason that Yves Saint Laurent once mused that he wished he had invented the blue jean. A well-fitting pair of jeans (preferably dark denim and boot cut) flatters most body shapes and can easily be dressed up or down depending on your mood. A great pair of jeans can be accessorized a million and one ways with what you already have in your closet.

4. CASHMERE CARDIGAN OR CREWNECK

A basic necessity for chilly restaurants and in-flight cabins. It's also the perfect companion for travel in colder climates.

5. BALLET FLATS

I love a 4" stiletto just as much as the next Louboutin-loving girl, but it's my ballet flats that I turn to time and time again for ease, comfort and weekend casual. There's a certain insouciance to the ballet flat that says, "clearly I know my way around the fashion block, but I just don't have to try so hard to look fabulous."

6. HIGH HEEL PUMPS

Whether peep-toe or classic, stiletto or chunky heel, a high heel pump in a neutral color (black, brown, navy or nude) will work well with all of your other wardrobe essentials.

7. PENCIL SKIRT

Much like the LBD, this item will take you from the boardroom to cocktails in style. It looks fabulous on all body types and is easily paired with a classic white shirt of cashmere sweater.

8. BLACK PANTS

Look for a slim fit and make sure the hem falls just an inch or so above the floor. And unless you are 6' tall and very thin, avoid too many pockets and pleats, as these can add bulk where we don't want it.

9. FITTED BLAZER

Your jacket should follow the silhouette of your body and accent the hourglass curve at your waist. It's the perfect piece to pair with your pencil skirt or black pants and a white shirt. Or make it more casual with a pair of jeans.

10. TRENCH COAT

This is one of those classic pieces that always seems to be "on trend." While Burberry is probably best known for their trench, there are many other brands who have created their own version of this staple. Check out Theory, Tory Burch, Zara, Kenneth Cole, Tahari and DVF. The trench coat has come to the rescue of many a "bad wardrobe" day.

Being chic isn't about having the most expensive handbag or wearing the latest trend. It's about being true to who you really are and feeling comfortable in your own skin. Real style comes from within. It's having the confidence to get organized, select items that you love and work for your body type and trusting your own creativity. If you feel great, then you'll look great—whether your outfit cost $100 or $1,000.

Now that's great style.

"

Style;
all who have it
have one thing:
originality.

DIANA VREELAND

WHAT IS A STYLE GUIDE?
(and Why You Need One)

A Brand Style Guide is a visual reference tool that displays how a brand presents itself to the world. We remember the most compelling brands because their presence is consistently defined by the repetition of the same logo, colors, fonts, icons and images. The style guide ensures brand consistency throughout everything you create—from business cards to ad campaigns, websites to social media posts.

Your style guide is the key to your brand identity. It is the visual piece of your brand handbook that explains exactly how your brand should be communicated across all mediums. It provides consistency and clarity — two key factors in building trust with consumers.

Your style guide should contain the following elements:

1. LOGO

This should include the proper size, proportion and placement of your logo, along with how NOT to use the logo.

2. COLOR PALETTE

The exact colors you have selected for your brand so that you can color match perfectly. You'll want to include hex and RGB codes for digital use, and CMYK and Pantone for print use.

3. FONTS

A good branding rule of thumb is to not have more than two (three maximum!) fonts for your logo design, website and printed materials—otherwise it creates visual clutter and confusion. Make sure you specify which font goes where—i.e. which one will be used for headers, which one will be used for body copy, etc.

4. ICONOGRAPHY

If you use an icon (or icons) as a part of your logo, then the correct usage should be included in your style guide—size, color, placement, etc.

5. PHOTOGRAPHY/IMAGES

If an image is used as a part of your logo, then as with iconography, above, you need to specify exactly how the image should be used (and NOT used), particularly in conjunction with your fonts and color palette. This is also a good place to specify the types of images that are appropriate for your brand and the type of mood and tone you want to set. Showcase a handful of images as examples of how you want your brand represented.

6. VOICE

What language best represents your brand? You'll want to revisit both your brand attributes and your brand personality to come up with a list of words that best communicate your brand voice (it may be some or all of these words combined). One way to do this is to come up with a list of "Words We Like" and a list of "Words We Don't Like" to best communicate your brand voice.

THE SHEBRAND
STYLE GUIDE

LOGO

VARIATIONS

CREATING COMPELLING BRANDS FOR WOMEN
AND THE COMPANIES THAT SPEAK TO THEM

BUILD A SMART BRAND WITH STYLE

COLOR PALETTE

PANTONE®
270 U

PANTONE®
273 U

FONTS

Didot

———

A B C D E F G H I J K L M N O P Q R S T U V W X Y Z
a b c d e f g h i j k l m n o p q r s t u v w x y z

Franklin Gothic

———

ABCDEFGHIJKLMNOPQRSTUVWXYZ
abcdefghijklmnopqrstuvwxyz

ICONOGRAPHY

The butterfly is a symbol of radical transformation. It also represents overcoming tremendous challenges and growing into something beautiful and free.

VOICE

SheBrand's Brand Personality is warm, intelligent, stylish yet accessible and feminist AF. We are your biggest cheerleader—like an older sister or best friend who wants to see you thrive. We are NOT stuffy, preachy or condescending, but we are a little bit badass.

PULLING IT ALL TOGETHER

YOUR BRAND HANDBOOK

"

Use your brains, your common sense, and do not become an object. The way you look is important, but who you are and how you project it is eventually *who you will become* and how you will appear.

DIANE VON FURSTENBERG

WHAT IS A BRAND HANDBOOK?

Your Brand Handbook can be presented in both hard copy and digital formats and it includes two parts:

1. The Foundation

A few pages to sum up what your brand is all about: your values, the promise you're making to your clients and customers, your mission, your vision for the future of your business, and more.

(If your brand was a tree, this section represents the strong, sturdy roots.)

2. The Style Guide

A list of important information and links that you'll want to have readily available. Things like: downloadable links for your logos and product photos, your official color palette and fonts, communication guidelines for emails and posts that go out to your audience, and other Brand Touchpoints, all organized neatly in one place.

(If your brand was a tree, this section represents the branches and leaves—everything your customers can see, touch, and interact with.)

Unfortunately, many people never take the time to put together a Brand Handbook. As a result, their brand feels scattered, their messaging is inconsistent, and aesthetically, they're all over the place. This builds confusion in customers' minds, and that's not what you want. Remember, a confused mind never buys.

CREATING YOUR VERY OWN BRAND HANDBOOK.

Now that you've completed the exercises in this Workbook, you should be able to put together your very own Brand Handbook easily. You've already done the work. Now, we're just summing it up all in one place.

You can fill out the next few pages by hand, or if you prefer to type, you can download a Brand Handbook template at: shebrand.com/style-substance-brand-handbook

KEEP IT CLOSE. REFER TO IT OFTEN.

Once you're done, I recommend storing your Brand Handbook in two places: one, printed and bound so that you've got a physical copy on your desk, and two, stored as a Word doc or PDF on your computer desktop so you can refer to it often.

I also recommend sharing your Brand Handbook with your team members, freelancers, contractors, or anybody else who's involved with your business, so that everyone's got the same information, and everybody's on the same page. This will prevent annoying (and often costly) inconsistencies, like having a virtual assistant use the wrong font for a newsletter, or having your graphic designer totally miss the mark with a new product label design.

STUCK? NEED TO MAKE A DECISION? LOOK TO YOUR BRAND HANDBOOK.

Whenever you're facing a dilemma in your business, large or small ("How should I write this new program description?" "Which photo should I choose for this post?" "Where should I focus my attention this month?" "What's the message I want to express in my TEDx Talk?") refer back to your Brand Handbook to guide you. It will keep you focused, clear, and consistent.

MY BRAND HANDBOOK

THE FOUNDATION

ABOUT

What's your story? What are your credentials? What gives you an edge on your competitors?

_____

_____

_____

_____

_____

_____

_____

_____

_____

_____

_____

_____

BRAND ATTRIBUTES

If you overheard people talking about you and your work, what are 3-4 words you'd want them to use?

BRAND PROMISE

What is the main promise you're making to your clients and/or customers? You can also think of this as your "end-game." What's the destination (feeling, achievement, situation, result) that you're guiding them towards?

_____

_____

_____

_____

_____

_____

_____

_____

_____

_____

_____

_____

_____

_____

_____

_____

MISSION STATEMENT

What is your greater mission? How are you changing lives and changing the world?

VISION STATEMENT

Where do you see your brand headed in the future? What will you have accomplished in five years? Ten years? Twenty?

BRAND PERSONALITY

If your brand were a person, what type of personality would she have? What's her vibe, spirit, and communication style?

TARGET AUDIENCE/IDEAL CLIENT

Who are you trying to serve? What do they want more of? Less of? What do they value?
Can you describe their lifestyle? Can you describe their fears, dreams, and goals?

STYLE GUIDE

Now it's your turn. In the space provided, fill in the information you'll use in your own Style Guide.

LOGO & VARIATIONS

Create a folder on your computer (or insert downloadable links) for all your company logos so you can grab them quickly whenever you need them. This will save you tons of time. No more frantically searching your hard drive trying to find a misplaced file!

PHOTOGRAPHY/IMAGES

Create a folder on your computer (or insert downloadable links) for your head shot(s) and any other photos/images you might need, like product photos, book photos, and so on, so you can grab them quickly whenever you need them.

COLOR PALETTE

Make a list of the colors that you'll use consistently throughout all of your Brand Touchpoints (website, business cards, emails, etc.). Put the name of each color and, if possible, the Pantone number or hex code. A hex code is a six-digit code that web/ graphic designers use to identify the exact color you want (the exact shade of lavender, teal, yellow, and so on). You can visit www.pantone.com and www.color-hex.com to find codes for every color in the universe.

FONTS

Make a list of the fonts that you'll use consistently throughout all of your Brand Touchpoints (website, business cards, emails, etc.). Ideally, you don't want to use more than two or three fonts for your materials.

ICONOGRAPHY

Is there a symbol or icon that represents your brand – or that you use as a part of your logo? If so, include it here.

VOICE

Write down the communication guidelines for your brand. For example, will you always start – or end – your emails in a particular way? Are there certain phrases you'll use often? Any phrases you'll never, ever use? You can imagine you're hiring a writer to work for your company – someone who's going to write blog posts for you, and social media posts, email newsletters, product descriptions, and so on. What are some of the voice/communication guidelines this person would need to know about? What is the tone you want this person to use in all of your brand communications? That's your voice.

I AM NOT AFRAID.

I WAS BORN TO DO THIS.

JOAN OF ARC

CONCLUSION

Beyoncé wasn't built in a day.

And you won't be, either. Your brand is an ever-evolving entity that takes time to marinate and develop. Clarity is a process. Consistency manifests over time.

Chanel, one of the most iconic fashion brands of all time, began with a single hat shop in Paris. The very first Starbucks opened back in 1971, and they didn't sell Frappuccinos or Pumpkin Spice Lattes or pastries back then, just plain coffee and tea. When Facebook launched, founder Mark Zuckerberg called the site "FaceMash" and the layout and functionality was completely different than the site we all know today.

The moral of these stories? Legendary brands are not born overnight. Empires are built one brick at a time. Logos change. Taglines change. Products change. CEOs evolve and grow, and their brands evolve, too. This is true for icons like Beyoncé, Chanel, and Facebook, and for your brand, too.

I encourage you to be open to experimentation and evolution, to be persistent, and most of all, to be patient. It may take one, five, ten years – or more – to build a strong, compelling brand with legions of loyal customers. It takes time, but your dedication will be rewarded.

BEFORE CLOSING THIS BOOK... TRY THIS.
I've guided you through many, many questions and exercises in this workbook. There's no need to complete all of them in one day, or even one week or month. Take your time.

If you're feeling slightly overwhelmed by all the material in this book, here's a "closing exercise" for you to try... sit down, set a timer for 30 minutes, and answer the following five questions. Write whatever comes to mind. Try not to edit or second-guess your instincts. Just write from the gut.

Even if you don't do anything else that I've recommended in this book, if you can answer these five questions, then you're already well on your way to creating a strong, compelling brand:

If you were the invisible woman at a party and overheard a conversation between an acquaintance and someone who was working with you, what are the three words you would want them to use to describe you?

What is the end result that someone gets from working with you? In other words, what is the value you provide them?

Why do you care about the work you do? Why does it matter?

When someone interacts with you in some way – visits your website, meets you at an event, hears you speak or works with you – what do you want them to feel?

How is the work you do different from others in your industry? Whether you are a coach, consultant, financial advisor or interior designer, there is something you bring to the table that no one else does. It is often a unique combination of your skillset, experience, education, personality, background or a different way of looking at things. What differentiates you?

THERE IS ONLY ONE *YOU*.

There will never be another you in all of history, space and time. You bring something to the table that no one else can. During the short period of time that you are living on this planet, it's your job to figure out what that "something" is and do it.

It's time to make your mark and make a difference. The more you own your personal power and bring it to the playing field, the more your brand will resonate with the people who are meant to work with you.

Whether your goal is to achieve "Bey-hive"-level fame, or simply sell more of your products and services and make a comfortable living, you hold in your hands the foundational tools to set yourself up for success.

As is always the case in life, the most fruitful path is one foot in front of the other, one day at a time.

You've got this.

NOTES

NOTES

NOTES

NOTES

NOTES

NOTES

NOTES

NOTES

NOTES

ABOUT LIZ

Liz Dennery Sanders is a brand consultant, creative director and the founder of SheBrand. With 20+ years of experience in branding, marketing, public relations and influencer outreach campaigns, she's known for her ability to select the words, images and packaging that bring brands to life, and for helping her clients to build intensely loyal, devoted fan bases.

In 2009, Liz founded SheBrand to provide women with tools to build strong, compelling brands. Through SheBrand, and through her involvement with organizations like Women in Need, Visionary Women and Step Up Women's Network, her mission is to help women rise higher – using their voices, growing their confidence, building their businesses, running for political office, and shattering glass ceilings and old perceptions about what a woman is capable of being and doing.

Prior to founding SheBrand, Liz ran her own PR agency, Dennery Marks Inc., for more than a decade, specializing in targeted media and celebrity outreach campaigns. She garnered millions of dollars in press value for her clients and helped them build relationships for their products and services with Hollywood celebrities like Halle Berry, Sharon Stone, Kendall Jenner, Kim Kardashian, Cindy Crawford, Heidi Klum, Gwyneth Paltrow, Marcia Cross and Kelly Rutherford. She has worked on brand development and influencer projects with individuals like Serena Williams, Jessica Alba and Garcelle Beauvais, and lifestyle brands that specifically market to women like Escada, Hale Bob and Elyse Walker.

Liz has been featured in *The Los Angeles Times*, *The Orange County Register*, *The Chicago Tribune*, *The Daily Beast*, *The Coveteur*, *Guest of a Guest*, *The Huffington Post*, *Good Morning America*, *E! Online* and *Access Hollywood*.

She's the author of *Style & Substance*, and the creator of Badass Brand, an online class for small business owners and service professionals who want to build an iconic brand that's clear, consistent, recognizable, adored and respected, just like Chanel, DryBar and Beyoncé.

Follow Liz on Twitter and Instagram for daily inspiration: @shebrandliz

Learn more about Liz at www.shebrand.com.

Made in the USA
Monee, IL
20 August 2020